Poems by

BRYAN BORLAND

My Life as Adam

 SiblingRivalryPress

ALEXANDER, ARKANSAS
WWW.SIBLINGRIVALRYPRESS.COM

Poems from this collection have appeared in *Ganymede*, *Breadcrumb Scabs*, *Velvet Mafia*, *vox poetica*, *The Foliate Oak*, *qarrtsiluni*, *Shape of a Box*, and *Young American Poets*. Gratitude to the editors.

Appreciation to Christopher Baxter, Loria Taylor, the late John Stahle, Philip F. Clark, Seth Ruggles Hiler, Annmarie Lockhart, Raymond Luczak, Emma Jean Matheny, Jessie Carty, Stephen Scott Mills, David Koon, and my family for their support.

Sibling Rivalry Press, LLC
13913 Magnolia Glen Drive
Alexander, AR 72002

www.siblingrivalrypress.com

ISBN: 978-0-9832931-4-9

First Sibling Rivalry Press Edition, March 2010
Second Sibling Rivalry Press Edition, May 2011

For the two men in my life
who were there first:

Glenn Borland
and
Jimmy Borland

CONTENTS

THE POEMS OF BRYAN BORLAND
Adam in Hindsight: God's Inconvenience

by Philip F. Clark

Who can tell how a poem is born to anyone, let alone those who are born to poetry itself? When does the process of "being" become self-recognition? In Bryan Borland's case, it is closer to the symbolic and sacred rib: ripped away to give life elsewhere, its loss provides not absence but insight. There is nothing less, but rather something larger. The new being is formed of words from the heart; the knowledge gained is the raw skin and bone of language. The body is renewed and written upon.

His poetry is a direct confrontation with all that we've taken for granted, in anything that we believe, and he throws back on us the reflections of a gay man in the process of making his own wide-eyed, questioning new Adam – his roving mind is God's ultimate inconvenience, as he runs full force from

...planting seeds of normalcy that never grew.

Normalcy is barren. Religion is questionable and foreign to a spirit and eye that has seen and felt something beyond the place that everyone else is telling you to look. Adulthood is reached by looking in the other direction. And Borland always does.

What good is a son who questions every commandment? This is poetry not only about being gay, but becoming gay. Finding voice in the body, the mind, and the spirit of complete refusal. In Borland's view of earthly delights, if we have no faith other than love, then that is all the faith we need.

To say these are love poems is to underestimate their intent. Here, love is where flesh converges with questioning: where a budding knowledge of being different is what is gladly bitten into – that sweet apple of the male body. It is gained in motel rooms, speeding cars, hospitals where friends lay dying. It is found in quiet

kitchens, stinking trenches, and crowded proms; on the mouths of
married men, in the arms of brothers, on the

> *...musty shirts stolen from locker rooms*
> *forced over feathered pillows that didn't love us back.*

The boys-becoming-men who populate these poems are tear-
stained, cum-stained, and shit-stained, all the fluids of no remorse.
Whether married or single, gay or straight, they are banded
together by need – which is sometimes love, but most often only
lust. Yet none of them bat an eye at love's lying condolences.
Unscathed by betrayal, they scrape up, wipe themselves off, and
move on, still sure that love is just ahead; that someone is always on
the way to them:

> *it is not good for man*
> *to be alone*

> *when he discovers his soul*
> *is between his legs.*

Borland is attuned to contemporary vernacular oracles,
Iraqed, Columbined, and 9/11ed to death, piping the heated mix of
dance and grunt, sigh and wish, headline news and sudden "tweet"
into poems that enjoy illicit readings. Somewhere, too, others are
under the covers with flashlights hoping to decipher in the dark
some explanation for all their sweating questions. But fuses are
also shortening. Why wait for something to happen? Make it
happen first:

> *It was easy to see why we'd pace like dogs*
> *who'd turned on their owners,*

> *the bloody fingers of blame pointing our way,*
> *the predictable story:*

the ones who everybody knew
got kicked in the gut

and would explode at any time
like dangerous, queer grenades.

What opens in these poems is a sense of surprise – at how wonderful it is to simply touch another human being. A world where sex is still contained to the flesh and the surprise of connection, the ardor of actually touching someone rather than "sexting" them in cyberspace. They recall a time

...when connections were made on the strength of a glance
not the invisible muscle of manic wireless signals...

The world's electric hum herds us into consciousness. The culture of the quick fix has become the culture of the quick fuck. Facebook has replaced the Good Book. Married men on the make on Sundays after church. Make no mistake, Borland understands and accepts the camaraderie of cyber-culture and its possibilities for fraternal auguries. It's a wide, sex-filled world out there, just waiting to be tasted. Press button, click, send. Who's online? Who's out there? Choices everywhere, but which to choose? But in the end, it's found lacking and devoid of what is sought after most: body-to-body, eye-to-eye connection. The conduits of such connection travel different paths in the lives of Borland's subjects: these are men who often have few choices at most. But the choices they make are at least truly their own. These are men who never go looking past their own backyards – a thrill and lack at the same time. There is the danger, too, of uncomfortable complacency.

Living in Arkansas, growing up where gay life was something rarely imagined –

Queer was a New York City thing...,

Borland's boys and men (versions of his experience) nonetheless learned to see through all the family secrets, learned the gestures of sexual recognition, and defied (and deified) the codes of religious upbringing in order to tear past the lies. This sensitivity to what was innate but unspoken leads them to erotic truth. The truth is not spoken so much as slept with. When bedded, the boys call all the shots. Ardent as well as urgent, these guys are not letting you off easy. They just don't have the time to waste. If you're lucky and you let them embrace you, you have a friend for life. Some of them never have the ability to feel, much less touch. But there is a craving for connection and completion.

For Borland, it is friendship that is the ultimate tribute; to stay the course with each other. It is what lasts through everything. Its reach is able to grasp glass from broken faces, and kiss damaged mouths, to take chances and risk being loved. It waits for you to come out of jail. It certainly is blood-brothered solid, even when time takes its toll and distance becomes unbearable. And if it succumbs to death, it does so in defiance and celebration. Borland is just behind the dark stare of AIDS, but still close enough to have smelled its hospitals, watched its ravages, lies, and betrayals of hypocrisy:

> *The priest due soon, your mother*
> *told me to say goodbye,*
> *that she'd like your family with you in the end.*
> *I wanted to ask her*
> *where she was at three in the morning,*
> *who changed the wet sheets,*
> *who held your head in your sickness,*
> *who brushed your hair away from your eyes*
> *and read you stories you memorized as a child?*
> *In my numbness*
> *I leaned down and in front of your father*
> *kissed you full on the lips,*
> *determined not to let you*
> *go over this edge alone.*

Friends also keep each other honest. In Borland's realm of friendship, there are acts of kindness that compel us to reconsider such things as orientation. His cohorts are often the same men who run around with the local girls, the same boys with whom he double-dates at the prom, the young hunks who regale him with pornography that he transposes good-naturedly into a simple acknowledgement of who the other is:

> *My straight friend,*
> *clumsy and thoughtful,*
> *embracing me*
> *before I could embrace myself.*

And too, the straight man who once loved him, now married and in another life. Years go by but time does not suppress a potent image of memory:

> *I'd watch him communicate patiently with*
> *his deaf younger brother, his rough hands*
> *transformed through sign language,*
> *a gentle education*
> *on the complexities of the world.*
> *These are my last memories of him.*

> *I picture him now guiding the new guys on*
> *how to operate the machines.*

> *I picture them listening.*

These poems are portraits in the best sense: visual omens in which we can read the faces that the words depict. We have a sense of their individual personas and colors – their climates changing with their moods, and their emotions changing as we look at them head on. As in every portrait, time is stopped at that instant that the face connotes all that language fails to provide. But Borland does both, letting language describe those instants of recognition, those sketches that in their quick and sure hand reveal something deeper than the surface. He shows us a rogue's gallery of men, all captured in that flash of insight that is both a mirror and a door.

Families are our sustenance and our gruel. Borland's family is no different. If he wages emotional wars with relatives, he also understands that they are no less enemies than they are friends. They provide us with their idea of Eden, but we often leave it, running. We are their inconvenience, too: we know too much, we've seen too much, we've heard too much. So why is everybody silent, Borland asks. He knows that once spoken, words cannot be taken back. He never takes back his, but there are small signs of peace in retrospect; a remembered instance of simple sharing:

Over milk we sang the day
as the dog beneath the table
licked greasy fingers and begged for more.
The taste was elegant to her tongue,
but we couldn't wait
for the store-bought cookies,
two a piece,
rationed sweetness,
fairly shared.
Three chairs pushed back,
we walked from the kitchen nourished and full,
but only now, Mother,
do I know why.

At the very least, families are where our lives begin. He concedes something to that. The roofs over our head, the food on the table, the listening ear when it was needed most: how does one not accord love to these things? How does one not attest that fathers still remain our ultimate battle: how to love them as we separate ourselves from them? How to let them be who they are until we can catch up as ourselves and recognize what poet Robert Hayden, in his poem "Those Winter Sundays," called, "love's austere and lonely offices"?

And one day we then come to our own loves, the brush with joy we experience when a life with a lover begins. The mundane acts of getting to know another person who is your other, your surfeit, your husband. Finally, husband!

We sleep in a tight squeeze
until we can afford
a larger bed.

Husband, dear,
why do you think I spend our pay
on exotic herbs
and good chocolate?

If every dime we save
is an inch you're apart from me in the night
our grocery lists will remain long,
our cupboards well stocked.

At the core of all of these poems is a deep, singular love that runs calm and steady through all the wonderful chaos of Borland's becoming a poet. The love of a brother lost too early gives rise to some of the most stunning poems in the collection. In the short period they shared, nurture is never farther than his embrace. That embrace takes the form of silence when necessary, but is never lessened by it. One can look to literary "influences" when considering the development of a poet, and Borland has them. But it is the nonverbal world that moved him most, that seeped into his consciousness and memory. The world inspired and weighted by a presence just out of reach – by time or circumstance – one soul always just ahead of the other:

I still wonder what he'd say, my brother,
who arranged my GI Joes in sexual positions,
who explained biology
with pornographic magazines,
who knew before anyone but left
before I could truly make an appearance.
When we'd play hide and seek as children
I always ended up in the closet.

He would help me out gently.

I think it was a sign.

A sign to save us, as we run from all our paradises and become complete and loving men. The love here is one of overpowering attention. We are often mirrors to each other as siblings; though lives separate and darken, we still encounter beauty:

> *I knew I was gay*
> *the year that he died.*
> *His room felt the way houses do*
> *when their families leave them,*
> *a cold and quiet winter with*
> *the curtains drawn.*

Poems of such self-examination are the product of what is imprinted at birth. What we are marked by, we are known by. Whether family, love, sex, or society, we have within us all some strand of being that persists. This persistence is why poets such as Borland continue to reveal the truth in front of us. In the end, what we are left with in these poems is the sense that nothing else matters except that truth: to one's self, one's life, and one's being. Bryan Borland has extracted in words the ability to see through the commonplace of lies – and not negating their uses – shows us that love is constantly a preamble to growing wiser and always an epitaph for understanding. We look forward with a look back, which is the only way we can turn towards love to begin with. We gather back everything and embrace what was once lost, or from which we tried to run away. Memory is our companion. Some heart is always beside us, remembering more than we can.

Philip F. Clark is the author and editor of The Artpoint *(http://theartpoint.blogspot.com), a blog that presents the work of artists in all mediums. A native New Yorker, he is also an Associate Director/Chief Analyst of Communications and Docketing for The New York City Law Department.*

MY LIFE AS ADAM

In the beginning, I was the first on Earth
to feel this way, born

from the dust of the ground, the salt
of my father, hungry for graven images of myself,

awakening from shameful dreams
ripping bone from my new body,

a boy carrying mankind's progeny
in sweaty psalms.

In the beginning, I tilled the garden, planting
seeds of normalcy that never grew,

ever-present voices inventing sin,
threats of banishment in booths meant for confession:

it is not good for man
to be alone

when he discovers his soul
is between his legs.

THE DEAD SEA SCROLLS

I kept them hidden from my mother,
the notes my brother left
in a shoebox under his bed,
mostly from his girlfriends, some
in his handwriting,
undelivered or unfinished.

I knew I was gay
the year that he died.

His room felt the way houses do
when their families leave them,
a cold and quiet winter with
the curtains drawn.

I read every one,
searching for an explanation,
trembling like a three-legged dog
who'd not yet mastered
the new distribution of weight.

EARLY VALENTINE

Sixth grade stands out,
with Jay and his late-eighties hair,

the first boy in our class to discover
gels and spray and bathroom mirrors.

He was mean to me, jealous
because I was smarter,

because I made an appearance
on the television news

delivering the weather into homes
of the pretty little girls he loved.

I faked the results of the science experiment
that won me small-town media acclaim.

I faked the Valentine I chose
for Jay that year,

Be My Friend
when *I'm Yours* hid in my backpack.

EDEN IN HINDSIGHT

When Eve and Adam reminisce on Eden
they do not recall mosquitoes
or how sometimes it wouldn't rain for weeks
and the fig leaves would brown and wither.

It wasn't all apples.

Their fallible memories omit
the bickering.
Adam forgets feeling
like the frayed rope in an egotistical tug-o-war.
Eve does not recollect
being kept dumb in lieu of defiance.

The moment some things are taken away,
they become paradise.

Barren trees grow green and strong
in mind gardens tended by
absent lovers.
Jealous gods become
protective fathers with time and mileage.
Revelation ugly turns to Genesis beautiful
in the drunken light of distance.

When Eve and Adam reminisce on Eden,
they do not recall snake pits or
rotting fruits.
They do not think of
the chill of winter on naked flesh or
trees of life guarded by
angry angels.

They do not remember
how free the wind felt
as they fell from grace.

ALTAR BOYS

With our legs
dangling
over an old wooden bridge,
he asks me if I ever pray.
The hot, sour smell
of the train tracks behind us
mixes with the scent of our stolen beer
and his cologne.
Through the darkness I
feel him studying me.
I think
Yeah I pray. You're here, aren't you?
but only mumble
"I guess."

QUEER PROGRESSION

Two twenty-something men on MTV,
a kiss behind apartment building bricks.
Queer was a New York City thing. I don't know
how many sidekicks slipped by unnoticed,

don't know when I began to pay attention to
bottom corner ads in the back of dirty magazines,
to junior high teases that hurt like gospel.
Manhattan skies were gray on television,

crowded, cold, body-heat breathing.
In Arkansas our winters were mild.
The Bible and TIME on our coffee table,
Ellen DeGeneres, *Yup, I'm Gay.*

I couldn't look her in the eyes.

We were always changing channels in my house.

ON DISCOVERING
A CHILDHOOD FRIEND IS GAY

When I discover a friend from childhood is gay
I ache for missed opportunities.
I ache because we created worlds together
but our bedroom walls were too thick
to hear growth-spurt whispers of the truth.
I ache because we lived three houses apart
and died adult deaths in boyhood isolation
smothering ourselves under lotion-damp covers,
raping ourselves with
makeshift dildos, musty shirts stolen from locker rooms
forced over feathered pillows that
didn't love us back.
I ache because the scars on his wrist should not be
a souvenir from 1991,
because twelve year olds should not
try to carve away their secrets,

because sleepovers could have been
so different.

TRICK

When I was young enough,
I met a man in a cheap motel.
He could have afforded much more
but he blew his wad on me.
My only moral dilemma
was where to spend the cash afterwards.
When the door closed behind me
he bought and discarded my fear.
He bought and embraced my nakedness.
Far from feeling used,
I felt powerful.
I felt beautiful.
I felt wanted.
I felt like a prince.
Far from feeling cheap,
my body felt expensive.
He bought my ego
like an eccentric man buys eccentric animals.
He bought my freedom and released me
like I'd been in bondage eighteen years.
He bought my apathy
for his jiggling belly on my back.
He bought my foolishness
and a rare youthful pause.
He bought my soul for thirty minutes.
His hands and wallet were heaven.
My price was god.
He tossed ten hundreds on the table
and told me to keep the room.
He assumed I was a professional.
The next day,
I bought Christmas presents.
I brought my brother video games.
I bought my mother perfume.

NATIONAL COMING OUT DAY, 1998

As a sophomore I skipped my classes,
hid in my dorm-room closet, lived on warm soda

and stale crackers and pissed in a cup
instead of walking down the hallway

or across campus, instead of making
myself an easy target for sniper glances

as deadly as a hatchet to my Southern-Baptist
cock. For twelve hours of daylight,

I stood mute, a boy petrified
of the monsters under his creaking bed,

of judgmental angels with letterman jackets,
of firing squad congregations, without even

a glimmer in the warzone of a country boy's brain
that one day, I'd feel October on my shirtless skin.

WEARING THE MASK OF CAIN

It was a hypothetical conversation
at a table of eighth-grade boys,

gun to our heads, choose
a relative to die.

I said my brother, who paid
more attention to his girlfriend,

who wouldn't share the telephone,
who played guitar too loud.

In the food fight that followed,
strawberry jam stained my fingers.

After his funeral,
I washed my hands until they bled.

MAGIC

From the front yard I leaned into his room
and watched him build to the climax
of his magic act, when he would vanish
from my world
leaving clouds of teenage apathy.

I could tell he'd rehearsed,
the same hands that made parts of me
disappear now working to
put things away neatly,

as if remaining was chaos
and leaving was order.

Outside the thorns of a rosebush
shared audience and hugged my legs
for dear life. We spun in circles
on our neighborhood stage as I begged

but he told me a magician
never reveals his secrets.

I knew the act had gone wrong,
the assistant sawed in two,
my skin punctured warm with a cut
that would leave a scar.

The pain was indefinable;
love was unrecognizable then.

MISSOURI

We fell asleep on the floor
with the stereo on repeat.
Meat Loaf's *Bat Out of Hell*
was an album we discovered
together, the same way
we discovered B-grade
horror movies
and mutual masturbation.
Your summer vacation
would be my agony.
I was fourteen and didn't
yet have a driver's license.
You were thirteen and
your parents lived
in different states.
When the music finished,
you left to visit your father
in Missouri
and never returned.

I have your baseball cap.

You have the guilt of a deserter
and a song stuck in your head.

IF NEXT YEAR HE GOES

On December 23, he turns seventeen
and the body count continues to rise.
I can barely picture him
behind the wheel of a car, let alone
operating a poorly-armored humvee.
I remember
horror-movie weekends,
frozen pizzas and chocolate pop-tarts,
paint-ball battlefields
where old clothes were the only casualties.
If, next year, he goes,
and I expect he will,
and Old Navy t-shirts and baseball caps
are traded for sand camouflage
and gas masks,
I worry the man who may return
the same but not
will harbor no trace
of the boy who went.
I hope that sudden desert blasts
do not replace flashes
of brotherhood
and that moments of sheer joy
survive the shrapneled limbs of suicide bombers.
How many young ones
must be molded into machines
before we collectively scream?
He sleeps down the hall
and already I miss him.

THE BOOK OF SAM

It was a turquoise motorbike
Sam told me to get on
in a challenge
more than a gesture of friendship.
With him, I found myself
so often saying yes.
I knew he'd smelled what I was
from the beginning,
the way wild animals smell
effeminate boys.
I could feel the danger
in our touching torsos,
my heart beating like
herds in chase. Unsure
what to grip, I clenched the rear
of the seat and nearly monkeyed backwards
when he accelerated the pavement
below to dust. I tried to concentrate
and balance myself but the dizzying warmth
of us pressed together, speeding like cheetahs
through the savageness of youth
distracted me and I forgot to be afraid.
We slowed long enough for me
to take an arm and guide it to his waist,
his stomach, one and then
the other until I was embracing him,
ten minutes that natural order
was interrupted.

SHOULDER

On the thirty-minute drive
between his bedroom and mine,
cloaked in the redeeming glow
of dashboard lights,
he spoke of his crush on
a classmate named Ben
and of how homosexuality
exists even in canines.

My straight friend,
clumsy and thoughtful,
embracing me
before I could embrace myself.

WIELDING DEAD BROTHERS

My secret weapon
was the blood clot that went
from his leg to his lungs.

Here, Quarterback.

I carried it in a holster just above my thigh.

Here, Homecoming King.

I carried it in a sheath wrapped tight
in curious adolescent flesh.

Here, All Star.

I carried it trigger-finger ready,
barrels in the mouths of kneeling boys who'd fit
into brother molds.

I was not afraid to use it.

Tears in my eyes
were a good touch. Even the quickest
of hearts could not resist slowing,
craving attention and spotlight,
the chance to play hero
in my Friday night
backseat fields, me
whispering

Here, Class President.
Here, Girlfriend's Brother.
Here, Neighborhood Badass.

In the crooks of their arms,

kissing their necks,
tangling them in my saline web,

I made them feel like men,

tasting sympathy
on their tongues,

never hesitation.

BITE

He tells me to use my teeth,
scrape the skin just barely,
just enough to

      make him feel it.

This from the boy who caught me like a hungry fish
on his shiny, perfect hook,
the minnow who swam like dinner in my bedroom oceans,
luring me with rubescent cheeks above and below,
the one who stood out
in schools of leaders and followers,
traveling, colorful clouds of tumbling positions.

This from the gentle boy whose quickening currents
I'd fought to slow into liquid forgetfulness
with nibbles so near to the back of his neck,
my stealthy arms drifting toward but never to, never around
his river-strong body.

This from the quiet boy washed to me
dripping and naked
but safe and willing along my crooked coastline,
carried along by my pleas for the pronunciation of pain
to float from his fluid vocabulary.

This from the trophy boy I saved from drowning,
into whose depths I'd so often dreamt
not of plunging piston-like with steam rising in
a delta vapor of swampy lust,
but of sinking sweetly and slowly to the bottom
with the carefulness of a trickling southern stream,

soft and with love.

This after he and I together tread bodies of sun-warmed water
undiscovered by all, untouched by any man,
the same boy with me as we reach the surface and gasp for air,
when there's not an inch of dry land in sight,
it is this boy who turns from tadpole to shark
and tells me

    make it hurt.

SUPPER

There was nothing fancy in the evenings,
meat and potatoes, salt and pepper,
something green cooked with bacon
for flavor.
Over milk we sang the day
as the dog beneath the table
licked greasy fingers and begged for more.
The taste was elegant to her tongue,
but we couldn't wait
for the store-bought cookies,
two a piece,
rationed sweetness,
fairly shared.
Three chairs pushed back,
we walked from the kitchen nourished and full,
but only now, Mother,
do I know why.

THE BOOK OF CODY

When we turned out the lights
he asked
y'wanna lick my ass?

God how I wanted
to slide down between
for a kiss.

Instead
I said no and
embarrassed us both.

PILGRIMAGE TO ARKADELPHIA

We lied to our parents
and drove too fast on an overnight trip
to revisit people and places from the limp
and leaning pedestals of his childhood memories.
I helped prop them by listening from
the passenger seat as he told of
what life was like before his parents' divorce, before
Pangea cracked and drifted apart and
distance as he knew it was created.

A hundred and twenty miles at fifteen is continental, when
crossing county lines seems foreign, when
feeling warmth through the holy shroud of tight denim
is enough to inspire acts of self-inflicted arson.

He knew I was in love with him. I'd hand him
painstakingly-crafted letters on folded notebook pages,
sweet words the same as any cheerleader would write to
the High School Golden Boy.

But he was never golden, this one.
He was a tarnished Boy God of sun-soaked skin,
North Carolina eyes, Arkansas tongue.
Southern Colossus chiseled in
Arctic-blue crystal and cloudy onyx,
black hair he or I would push away from his eyes,
black heart that in private pumped lava
just for me. He was
a chest just beginning to define itself,
to define my thoughts and my
slow unfolding.

He was lips wet with spit I craved
and chipped teeth sharp and
almost a man.

I remember the moment I acknowledged
I was aroused by thoughts of kissing him,

him,
another *he*,

when before it had been the
bare bone basics,
sex raw and rough, like boys with dirt-stained knees wrestling with
no hint of softness or intimacy.

My hand moving across
the newness of his pectoral muscles,
it was the same as
two fifteen-year-olds driving
their first hundred miles in the dark.

When we made it,
he showed me his old house
but couldn't remember what he'd really come to see.
One in the morning with nowhere else to go
we parked under an overpass and made
peace with geography.

When he looks back,
I'm sure I'm not the jewel
in the crown of his youth
but for that year
I was queen in his kingdom.

I still carry the title of royalty.

THE BOOK OF ERIC

I was attracted to the way he smelled in
afterschool camouflage as we kneeled
in autumn fields of easy targets.
Six months and twelve days made him wiser,
his little brothers made him adored.
I turned blind eye when he kicked dogs,
when he turned bully and left bruises and
holes in the wall. His whiskey-breath gave
me thirst to become predator,
crawling through the blankets just as we'd
crawled through mud to shoot arrows
at doe and fawn. This wasn't me but

I learned from watching.

Afterwards, I played dead against the
softness of his bed. Here he was clean,
toothpaste and soap having rid him of the
blood from his slaughter.
I wanted to kiss this part of him,
to bathe in his innocence. Instead
there was no tenderness.
He used what I gave,
my body, my dead brother's
hunting bow and knives,
skinning his game after
every kill. He took
what he could get, but then

so did I.

INTRODUCTION TO EVE

I was a procrastinating pussy,
loitering round that smiling mound
of flesh as long as I could,
listing reasons not to enter just as I'd
stood freshman-awkward the first day of school.

I was labia leery,
allowing her wrist to grow weary of masturbating me.
She wore scrupulously-selected bra and panties,
I wore off-brand emperor's clothes of virility,
both of us naked of excuses and delays.

I owed it to her because
she listened when I suggested she should cut her hair short,
because she wore unisex fragrance I bought her,
because with my eyes shut tight her body
bled into hallway boys and Jonathan Taylor Thomas.

The same way a child
eats his vegetables and cleans his plate,
I held my breath and paid my dues, carrying
the story of my debt and her satisfaction
like a convict proud of a jailhouse tattoo.

BLOOD

I passed time in math class and marching band
watching handsome Cain relate to handsome Abel
with nuzzles and punches, memorizing them like
infallible geometric proofs, following off key to their
perfectly tuned trumpet and saxophone.

They shared hard features, jagged noses, blue eyes.
They shared my attention like family. They wore
birthright uniforms of gold and brown I admired
with jealous froth at the corners of my hungry mouth,
only-child quiet and waiting.

When God invented brothers
he intended for them to be one year apart.
It pained me to think
they could destroy one another, that the sun
could go dark and take along the moon,

I couldn't stand to see something so beautiful collapse
so I offered myself, my jaw for their fists,
absorbing their fate so they could survive,
Cain and Abel, living happily ever after,
drops of heredity running down my grateful chin.

PROM NIGHT

In our tuxes we cleaned up good,
scruffy sixteen and seventeen
scrubbed away to reveal young men,
we could have been brothers

waiting for our dates, two girls who loved us
who would eventually make grand entrance
as costumed women in silver and gold
dashing my thoughts of their abstinence,

she held my sweating hand too tight,
hung her splendid expectations around my neck,
choreographed each slow dance turned painful toe step
until we fell into her sister's bed and she made love

while I made the best of things,
our rooms separated by a wall of expectations,
I could hear his grunts and the cries of a sofa, my eyes focused
on two black coats intertwined on the floor.

ATONEMENT

We drove two hours to
thank the nurses after he died.

Because I saw a cloud
in the shape of a red-tailed hawk,

I believed God could hear
my thoughts. I was ashamed

that I couldn't stop being
a thirteen-year-old boy

even on the day we buried him.
With his razor blade I cut

a cross in the palm
of my guilty hand. That night

I thought of Shane Abbott's lips
and burned in my bed.

TIME MACHINE

We almost feel cheated, my generation. Our sexual revolutions
were broadcast with a two-second delay, streamed live but muted.

We've never seen glory holes, those Swiss bank accounts
of gay passion. Our lovers were never hung like disco balls,

there were never only dark rooms, back alleys, winding trails,
bathroom stalls for two, some warehouse turned nightclub,

back when we always took him home, took him somewhere,
took him in with a welcome mat of wicked raw skin,

before death rode into bloodstreams like a horse into Troy,
before the world was smothered in spermicide and latex,

when we could still snort lines of strangers' sweat,
when we had to work for it, for everything,

when connections were made on the strength of a glance
not the invisible muscle of manic wireless signals,

before fevered afterglow was replaced by a sickening regret,
before red ribbons there was red-hot and dirty love, baby,

when the only question to be asked
was hey man, top or bottom?

when we were cultured but not pop culture,
when we were corner-bar cowards or front-page courageous,

when we weren't blowjob bulimics,
when we swallowed and didn't count anything.

SIMON

When Simon's body was found
three weeks after his death
no one claimed his remains
so he was cremated,
his ashes sealed in a hazardous-waste bag
and buried, forever separate from the dirt
in which he rests.

There was no dignity.

Simon,
near twenty years you've been at peace
but apart
from the earth in which you lay.

I want to find your grave
and dig at it with my bare hands.

I want to tear with my teeth
at the confines that keep you
from returning to the soil.

I want to kiss your ashes
then take them
to places I imagine you loved
and let the wind carry them
to the cool touch of glistening rivers,
to the feet of New York sunsets,
into crowds of young men
in fine clothes, in long lines,
who will breathe you in,
feel your spirit
and remember your name.

I want to release them

into the fresh air
where they will float
and shimmer
and finally fall on life again,

and there, Simon,

you will have your dignity.

THERE WAS A MOMENT OF TENDERNESS

There was a moment of tenderness
that returned with the smell
of the dentist, sterile metal and blood
and I thought of the foolish night
he drank his way into a telephone pole,
the bone of teeth breaking into pieces
that proved he was handsome even
in fragments. After his surgery,
I skipped school to drive him home.
In the cold, broad daylight
the warmth of his hand startled me.
It was the medication talking
or maybe I misheard
when he slurred words
that made us equals.
It was weakness
when he offered me his wounded smile,
how I sped from validation,
and returned us to familiar territory,
stories of sex with his girlfriend
while she was on the rag.

PHILISTINES FALLING

After church we tore off our
starched-white buttons ups and felt
temptation circle baptism
like two oil-slicked gladiators.
He didn't understand that wrestling was fake,
that love didn't have to sting
so I took elbows to the heart,
his leaps of faith off the top
of the old leather sofa where
our bodies made flesh-colored crosses
against the hard-wood floor.
I guess in size, I was Goliath to
his David, our weapons always drawn
halfway through our battles.
He fought like God was on his side,
violent to cover up
the softness of busted lip kisses
on the napes of sore necks.
I never pushed back, not like I could have,
never fending off his stones
thrown like alabaster angels,
submitting to his slingshot eruptions,
the giant falling at foot of a boy,
delivered, every time,
to Jerusalem.

GRAPES ARE THE PERFECT FOOD

was what we said to each other at
tense moments, which might have been

often, which might have been
the whole relationship, how many years

I've forgotten but I do remember
holding hands in public, or how

we'd order an appetizer at a restaurant
and she'd serve me before herself.

If it weren't for the sex
we might have made a go of it, lasted

beyond those early college classes
where I learned Christianity

was not the only religion, where
a boy named Jonathan turned me on

to matzah brei and kugel
and I couldn't get enough.

THE WAY TO A MAN'S HEART

My grandmother had never pumped gasoline.
I was seven years old
and watched as she asked a young mechanic
for help. He obliged, under the spell
of her low-country elegance
that stood out like white gloves
against the Arkansas delta mud.
Before we drove away,
she thanked him profusely. We returned
the next day with garden vegetables
and cornbread that left him
licking his lips.

She was already pregnant
when she met my grandfather,
something we didn't know
until she saw Myrtle Beach
from her nursing home window.
When I packed her things,
I found handwritten recipes,
notes on how much, how long,
scribbles of kitchen trials and errors,
menus of Christmas Eves and Father's Day feasts.
She'd taught herself to cook
and repaid him with chicken fried steak.

MARKS OF THE BEAST

Unpacking the campsite, we discovered with
shrugged shoulders the deliberate accident of

one sleeping bag forgotten. Three days of rain
had left the world dirty, our tingling fingers

snailing muddied trails behind everything
that we touched. I watched him

ignite the fire with kindred kindling, saw
the heat coax away clothing as

light melted into a slow moving pendulum
of purrs and prayers. At dawn,

when the blaze fell to ashes and soot
and we were boys again,

the cool, gray birth of morning showed us
the marks remaining from hours before,

our bodies tattooed in the night we became tigers,
one stripe for each claw and grasp.

AUTUMN

You never had a chance,
barely bone and mass
of dark hair like your mother,
my biological proving ground,
the sum of two mistakes, the
subtraction of possibility,
for this you suffered an end before you began.
I was not consulted or considered,
what value is the opinion
of a nineteen-year-old father?
You were to be a woman,
you were to be a queen,
but then you weren't to be at all,
not a memory or a cry,
not a political statement but a life inverted
and suctioned away. Our stupidity
was the death of you. The first
winds of October carry your name,
this world without dirt to cover your remains,
empty of a ghost to haunt two fools
who invented and erased you.

THE BOOK OF DAVID

He's divorced and remarried now, blue collared factory slave
in Mississippi somewhere, shackled to the second shift, daily
repetitive movements undoing history,
heat and grease replacing the smell
of freedom at sixteen,
of my bedroom in November, my parents off
chasing Rolling Stones.

He corrected me when I sang "bright red" instead
of "flat bed" Ford in "Take It Easy,"
said to treat it like a popsicle then
let me lay my head on his stomach

(most straight boys don't).

So many men but he was the only one who
took the time to teach me.

I'd watch him communicate patiently with
his deaf younger brother, his rough hands
transformed through sign language,
a gentle education
on the complexities of the world.
These are my last memories of him.

I picture him now guiding the new guys on
how to operate the machines.

I picture them listening.

WEEDS

They populate the soil
in our front yard
alongside
the marigolds and roses,
pretenders,
trying to blend in,
sometimes succeeding.
Sometimes they grow taller
than their counterparts,
haughty and proud
to have survived
another weekend.
I eyed them wearily at first,
taught that
if you let one in
others are sure to come,
schooled that
they will taint the rest,
stain the innocent seedlings
and shade the truly deserving
from God's gaze.
It is perhaps
a mark of my own kind heart
I pay them no mind
another Saturday morning,
let them flaunt
their wild difference
one more week.

HOLDEN

The hospital room was too white,
you never liked white
so I filled it with balloons and flowers and
photos from our home,
with clothing you wouldn't need
and a painting we'd bought in New Orleans,
the cats of Jackson Square
holding vigil from the corner.
Your sister said the apartment must be quiet with just me,
that I must be relieved
to not have the burden,
that I could have your larger bedroom
if I chose to stay.
The doctor gave you, at best,
two days,
the time it took for us to fall in love. You liked to say
God pushed us off the cliff together,
the only one I knew
who made Catholicism
guiltless.
The priest due soon, your mother
told me to say goodbye,
that she'd like your family with you in the end.
I wanted to ask her
where she was at three in the morning,
who changed the wet sheets,
who held your head in your sickness,
who brushed your hair away from your eyes
and read you stories you memorized as a child?
In my numbness
I leaned down and in front of your father
kissed you full on the lips,
determined not to let you
go over this edge alone.

FLAWED FAMILIES IN BIBLICAL TIMES

They're wonderful now but
when I told them I was gay,

my mother demanded God's reasons
for striking her grandchild-bearer dead,
manly loins fertile and righteous impeded
by my barren inclinations, her last straight hope
zooming past as she traveled
the stages of grief from the passenger seat,
my future like a tornado-ravaged town
with collapsed houses on the bodies
of grandsons and granddaughters,
crumpled white picket fences wrapped around the dead who
looked like Tom Hanks in *Philadelphia*.

My father took the proactive approach
and said if I tried I could find a butch woman
with a mustache or a petite little thing,
small-chested, like a freshman,
he could coach me around the bases,
close your eyes, son, and you'll never know.

My grandpa spoke of it
with the hushed words of a repressed war memory,
I was Hitler, I was Mussolini, I was Tojo and Konoe.
He saw me in grotesque scenes with a fat man and a little boy,
pink triangles lost on his sensibilities.
I was Hiroshima aftermath to his peacetime America,
pacific-rim foreign on toes farm-kid strong,
the flag at the post office flying half mast while
taps played solemn and survivors wept.

My grandmother didn't change at all,
stringing me out with sugar and butter creamed together
until I saw visions of her worshiped in another time,
a one-named siren in a bar surrounded by my people,
dirty jokes and colored hair,
God we would have loved her.
I think that homosexuality is genetic,
a decadent recipe passed down to
diabetic queens of the family.
I never went hungry.
Thank you, Grandma.

I still wonder what he'd say, my brother,
who arranged my GI Joes in sexual positions,
who explained biology
with pornographic magazines,
who knew before anyone but left
before I could truly make an appearance.
When we'd play hide and seek as children
I always ended up in the closet.

He would help me out gently.

I think it was a sign.

WHEN I WAS THE PHOTOGRAPHER

I took too many photographs of him,
asked him to smile too many times,
caught him by surprise, from behind,
burst of light in the dark
or an eye-squinted click in an iris-searing sun,
too many finger-ready moments,
too many
two-dollar wooden frames
meant to keep him
on a shelf,
too many
beautiful backdrops, beautiful excuses,
too many timers set,
holding him with muscled arms
expecting explosions to
disintegrate Saturdays mornings
into dust and wind,
and so when I was the photographer
there were albums of us,
four-by-sixes and polaroids to thumb through
to animate his lips, to make him say my name,
to make him say things maybe he really said,
but when he goes,
when he went
and when he's gone, I'm left
behind the lens
as if I never looked and saw him,
as if the flash never took
and the negatives were exposed.

THE LION'S DEN

The first time I walked into a gay bar
I felt like a piece of meat,

not raw, dripping red, but
a prime cut cooked

to a juicy medium rare,
and every man in sight was doomed,

watching the clock,
waiting for their last meal,

a blue-eyed boy perfectly seasoned,
aged twenty-two years.

THE CRUSADES

-I-

It begins
when my friend comes home from the war,
a line that feels wrong present tense,
the battles before saved for school books
and the far off stares of dying grandfathers,
seen in the weather-wrinkled trigger fingers
of aging uncles,
in yellow-paged poetry
with cadence rhythms in the distant behind,
in mythological terms like
foxhole or Vietnam or quadriplegic,
in inconceivable notions
like life before one's own birth
or the amputation of a leg.

War was not something real to us,
my buddies, my classmates.
Desert Storm, even,
we didn't flinch,
the landscape unaltered with
our mouths agape in little-league patriotism,

our entertainment the cable news loops:
black and green gunfights unfolding
like sheets dirtied by adulthood then
washed by mama
clean again.

-3-

Once-a-month weekend marches
paid for college and cars,
the military as touchable
as plastic childhood figures melted on
Georgia summer dashboards
or lost like make believe as we became men,
but then the call came
and little brothers and sisters lined up,
dutiful teenage tanks of bone and flesh and gun,
we saluted them goodbye and they just
disappeared.

Some of us followed
or had gone in the early days,
as weeks stretched into oceans
and aircraft carriers left and returned,
sometimes heavier with guilt or pride,
sometimes lightened by one less soldier,

one hundred less soldiers,

four thousand less soldiers.

When my friend comes home from the war,
when they all come home from the war,
when he's debriefed and declassified,
when he's given directions to the VA and
diagnosed a survivor,
when afterwards he sits with me at the bar,
sandscars hidden by civilian clothes,
an invisible flag draped over
shoulders forced broad and muscular,
I recognize the same unseen grip
squeezing silence into his throat,
the same stare of my grandfather in his screaming eyes,

so we drink
and toast his return with round after round,
laugh at jokes but don't speak of where he goes
in the punishing seconds between stories,
between step and blast or
life and death.
We don't acknowledge how his hands shiver in
nighttime deserts of collateral memory.
We pretend not to notice the changes,
the explosions of epiphany that come,
how now we understand
the chill of winter
and war's lingering moan.

THE BOOK OF BRANDON

His intellect did not pretend to fit
into the definition of his heterosexual
abdomen. We sat outside
with plastic cups of cream soda
and vanilla vodka, an odd combination,
not the usual Jack and Coke or
beautiful and dumb.

I remember his blond locks
but not his last name.
I remember confessing to him
I thought he was attractive
and blaming it on the spirit
when he replied *thank you.*

I remember the sadness I felt
when she spoke of his habits
like a terminal diagnosis.

I knew he had days to live.

SEASON OF REVERSALS

Dogs were not allowed in my grandmother's house
but Buster was there on December 15, 1992,
when I knew before my parents
my brother was dead.

He was a fox terrier, pure breed black
and white, who jumped higher
than I was tall and sneezed
when you commanded
him to speak.

The bathroom floor was carpeted.
I lingered there with
my arm around him
listening to my grandmother
lose a grandson through
the telephone.

My parents didn't know
I knew. When they returned
from the hospital
I met them in the driveway
to spare them the pain
of walking through the door
wondering how to tell me.

That morning
I saw my father cry
and a dog sleeping
on an antique sofa.

SPEAKING IN TONGUES

Between gulps of syllables
you said you wanted to speak my language,
the coded initiation to our lesson
that would leave nouns and adjectives
covering my body in your slanted handwriting,
the roughness of your voice,
the words "cocksucker" and "faggot"
lost in translation,
my burning ears
heard "baby" and "please."
With your penis in my mouth
it always seemed I held the power
of vocabulary.
You slapped my face,
I felt a caress.
You pulled my hair like a proud older brother.
"Swallow it bitch" was a love note I kept
for years
folded in my back pocket.

THE BOOK OF DMITRI

To call it a book is a misnomer,
more like a trashy romance novella
we all read on park benches
then hid in our designer man-bags
when we'd return from trick lunches.
This is what I remember
of Dmitri, what we all remember
of Dmitri: we fell for his thick
accent, the - *no?* - he'd kiss gently
onto every sentence. We told our
girlfriends about his traveling tongue,
took pleasure in their jealousy
as it spread like communism
over the Eastern European maps
we unfolded in public libraries
just to appear knowledgeable
of his geography. We swooned
when he promised to take us
to Pitsunda, the place he described
as paradise, then swallowed him
at his strong tsar-command
like the vodka shots every bartender
gave him for free. When acquaintances
peppered their sentences
with Russian words, we shook off
any thought of coincidence. Surely
there was more than one
young homosexual named Dmitri
in Little Rock, Arkansas,
who taught Southern boys like us
to say *Pah-ka, moya lee-u-bov.*

LEVI

I want you.
I want you like politicians want public office.
I want you like Alaskan hunters want moose.
I want you like teen lovers want abortions.

I've wanted you since
you were propped on stage
at the Republican National Convention
looking like a donkey
in elephant skin.

My god, that tusk.

I want you like
I wanted all the dumb jocks,
the ones delighted to discover
their strength at the polls
within certain demographics.

I want you like you want fame,
like the media wants mistakes,
like babies' mamas want child support.

I want to see Russia from your crotch.

WALLOW

We've tasted the fruit,
cherry-sweet tree-jewelry
eaten and admired from the ring fingers
of husbands' husbands and wives' wives.
Now you'll
pick through our shit to
prove you can take it away again,
dirty hands change nothing,
not the honey lingering in our mouths,
not the fires of compassion
lit and burning in the bellies of new
and newer generations,
not family histories already written
that read collectively and convincingly
I do.

LIKE ELVIS AND PRISCILLA

Like Elvis and Priscilla we married in Vegas,
exchanging fifteen dollar rings in
matching pinstripe pants, wrinkle-free shirts
complimentary yellow and pink
and white ties that blew in the desert wind, too elated
to stay flat on bellies full of expensive buffets.
Our airplane trembled with pre-wedding jitters
on our descent into Nevada.
Witnesses cheered as we rolled to a halt
and he and I walked down the aisle
arm in arm to piped in sounds
of *Love Me Tender.*

The closest we ever came
to having a three-way
was in the spa of Caesar's Palace, where
an impersonator offered his microphone
for a lip-synched performance. When neither of us
had the nerve for sexual karaoke, he grew
impatient and strutted away.
We spent the afternoon
in open towels running though the steamy maze
like two shirtless southern children.
We were innocent together,
holding hands at the altar,
smiling on the strip with our names in lights,
two boys each other's best men,
ignoring big brother
and the mother of the bride next in line
who wouldn't know love if it fell from the sky.

IF ERIC AND DYLAN HAD CHANGED THEIR MINDS

They assumed Eric and Dylan were gay
or in the least had homosexual tendencies,

not the Columbine kids,
in crossfire cafeterias or under table-trenches,

but the media
and America followed,

to the point where the murderers became Bonnie and Clyde,
french kissing each other goodbye,

sharing spit
like plans to kill.

But Eric and Dylan
were not gay

and if they had changed their minds
they would have told you so and laughed.

It was easy to believe,
to make asses out of you and me

with the Colorado sunset dripping
a flamboyant red,

it was easy to comprehend
that the oppressed would

snap like a spinal cord meeting the spray
of a sawed off shotgun.

It could have been us,
running through the hallways, armed to the teeth,

up and down the stairs,
these make believe killers

the newspaper dreamed up,
punched in the face for puberty,

our wrists limp from never hitting back,
our bombs internal, lacking biological choice.

It was easy to see why we'd pace like dogs
who'd turned on their owners,

the bloody fingers of blame pointing our way,
the predictable story:

the ones who everybody knew
got kicked in the gut

and would explode at any time
like dangerous, queer grenades.

THE LEVITE

My husband says I don't talk about him,
but thirteen years isn't enough for a lifetime

of conversation. How many times can I repeat
that I opened his Christmas presents

and carried the television from his room
with the strength of a pallbearer,

that I traded his belongings for the attention
of undeserving boys and that sometimes

I dream of kissing him?   There are things
I will not say, that I shape his ghost

into convenience, that I am not
the wounded sibling but

the grave robber who builds poetry
with his brother's bones.

ANGELS OF CHERNOBYL

They pay money to see a gaping wound
in the city, Ground Zero, New York,

where camera flashes confuse visitors,
whether to smile in the photographs

they ask strangers to take. Most do.
In the Lower Ninth, tour buses

idle at shotgun houses with death
painted on abandoned front doors.

I dated a boy once whose left arm
had been mangled in a car accident.

In bed he shyly asked me to kiss
his scars and shook in climax

at my breath against his skin.
He doesn't resurface often,

but from time to time I receive postcards,
the last from Ukraine, a picture

of a nuclear winter snow angel
I pressed gently to my lips.

THE BOOK OF JOSHUA, EPILOGUE

I browse the wedding registry and see
nothing of him in lists of
soft linens, stainless steel,
unbreakable dishes,
reliable appliances.

I see his new life framed in
matching patterns and
perfect pairs,
things he'd never want,
an inequitable trade,

me

for a wife
and a toaster.

THERE SHALL BE NO GODS

Right click
and he's ours,
pulsing pixel pseudonyms
like Cole and Kaden,
where all it takes is a dog tag
to convince us not to ask or tell.
We know them
like we know our own right hands,
the appendix scar,
the hairs of the forearm,
the shoe size. We know
their sins, saved (or lost)
forever on digital lenses,
on disc or drive stained
with drops of our souls,
our moments of passion
timed to the minute and the second
their muscles clench
in ways we've memorized.
They are as intimate to us
as old lovers, boyfriends,
the first kiss, the first time we entered
our credit card information,
the recurring monthly charge we forgot
to cancel. They are the Brents,
the Pierres, the young gods
like Holmes and Noll before,
the shrines to bodies
we'd pass on the street
and never recognize fully clothed.

SALVATION

Yesterday I told my mother
not to feed the strays.

This morning the cats cornered
a spider beneath my feet,
escaping their toying claws
in bouts of lucky last stands.
Even I was surprised
when I cupped it softly
in my hands and pardoned it
with a gentle brush
into overgrown nepeta.
The cats disagreed but
surely something that fought to live so hard
deserved reprieve.

I am my mother's son.

OUR MARCH

marching marching 1-2-3
marching marching bryan and me

marching marching 1-2-3
marching marching bryan and me

In between the earliest memories
of blue pajamas
and watchful cocker spaniels
I can feel myself
hoisted up and held against his shoulder,
moving circularly around the house,
a traveling pedestal
and I, the golden child,
his fathering voice
counting me
to a toddler's sleep.

marching marching 1-2-3
marching marching bryan and me

marching marching 1-2-3
marching marching bryan and me

Those words
set the rhythm
of my life,
of our relationship.
Those words
were my beautiful introduction
to poetry,

were the hammer and nails
that built my confidence,
my recognition and my definition
of unwavering love.

marching marching 1-2-3
marching marching bryan and me

marching marching 1-2-3
marching marching bryan and me

I know no greater gift to you, Father,
than to tell you
I remember our March,
that
in battles yesterday and yet to come
I have continued and will continue
to walk in the rhythm you taught,
and that never
for one second have I felt
alone,

that
every decision you ever made
     for me
was correct.

GRAPES OF COMFORT

Feeding my husband grapes
on a Sunday afternoon road trip,

to my sixteen-year-old self
who planned funerals instead of weddings

I want to show him this image
and tell him life will be sweet.

FAG/HAG
for Loria

I had no will and she had no grace.
We never went
to prom together.
There was no serious talk
of a child.
She never wanted
in my pants
and don't dare call her
a hag,
delegated to a secondary syllable,
a slur's tagalong.
Strong,
beautiful,
independent, yes
but never a hag.

-

We don't hug
or coddle each other
with concern flowery like
the mumus her grandmother gives as gifts to
females of the family,
with empty questions like
how are you or wastes like
good morning or good night.
We much prefer to mingle in
the socially-awkward humour of quirkiness, to
mangle and disable what we remember of
sign language and past friendships that couldn't survive
us, misfingerspelling witty one-liners
about existence or God's girl-like clingy need
for praise and validation,

to send or receive the
occasional text message,
are you going to hurt yourself today,
usually content with the quick response,
absolute and believable.

\-

The day before her thirtieth birthday
she gave me a gift:
the dented casing of a bullet
gingerly resting on her doorstep.
She called me, amused.
I was expecting this,
she said. I guess this means
my youth is truly dead.
She knows
it's not that I enjoy her tragedy
but that I enjoy her reaction to tragedy,
the chemical response in her brain that says
when life hands you lemons
laugh because
you're allergic to lemons
and now parts of you will surely swell.

\-

She bites into war stories like I bite into a cheeseburger,
her salty grease the proof of pain beyond herself,
she hasn't eaten in days, books double stacked around her,
we joke about it the way we always do with
pathology or cholesterol,
we laugh at the horror,
instead of acknowledging
it's just another way
of almost cutting herself in two,
I dip mine in ketchup

as she sinks her teeth
into more red meat.

--

When she takes her Ambien early
and calls me to say, slurring her words,
she's watching infomercials
and parading about
in a t-shirt and high heels to strengthen her calves,
I tell her it's perfectly normal -
perfectly normal in the context of
sleeping medication
and a deep love of shoes.

--

She asked me
twelve years after graduation
if I'd fooled around with Michael.
Of course I did, I replied
and she was jealous.
He had a shirt that said
must be this tall to ride.
She missed it by an inch.

SHOPAHOLIC

We sleep in a tight squeeze
until we can afford
a larger bed.

Husband, dear,
why do you think I spend our pay
on exotic herbs
and good chocolate?

If every dime we save
is an inch you're apart from me in the night
our grocery lists will remain long,
our cupboards well stocked.

SONS OF ABRAHAM

My grief grows with the years. I count
seventeen Octobers come and gone,

imagine a green-eyed boy
with hair the color of straw,

wooden walls sturdy on branches
long since chopped and used

for firewood. The older I get,
the more aches and pains: a nephew

and a treehouse, these things
my brother would have made.

THE BOOK OF ANDREW

The Lion King ends with Simba, the father,
mate at his side, cub at his feet.

I've known you since you
dreamed of a mane,

since your roar was a mew
and you pounced on your own tail.

I see you now with your son,
the man of the pride

nurturing that lucky boy
with gentle paw, my friend,

who maybe, instead of Simba,
was Mufasa all along.

WATCHING BROKEBACK MOUNTAIN IN LITTLE ROCK

White-haired ladies wear their Sunday best
next to husband and wife sharing the buttered body of Christ,
a teenage boy with the beginnings of a beard
shuffles anxiously in
stadium seating stiff as a church pew,
the makeup of parishioners
like a sanctuary on Christmas Eve,
unfamiliar faces but welcome nonetheless.

In Arkansas we see two men kiss
and turn away. There's no
affection on rural streets,
just pickup trucks and
rednecks on our breath.
In the temple of theater,
we are studied, two men
sitting too close, legs touching the way
our hands cannot.
We watch and recognize,
tune out the action movie stigmata
bleeding through the walls.

THE BOOK OF RICKY

He went to prison
for beating his daughter.
The irony was that, as a boy,
I wrote stories
where he saved his brothers
from an abusive stepfather,
where he wore the literary robes
of a teenage Jesus, heartthrob beautiful
with a tendency toward sacrifice.
As an adult,
he doesn't walk on water any more
than he did when we were children.
I no longer write him
as the hero of my daydreams.
Instead, I print his mugshot and
masturbate over his face.

KINK

After seven years together,
we keep things spicy.

I am not referring to the
great jalapeño indiscretion
of 2006,
suffice to say
sex and salsa
do not mix.

We've worn
handkerchiefs of many colors,
baseball caps turned backwards,
pants around our ankles
on old country roads,
on busy freeways,
on his brother's kitchen floor.

We still hit
triple plays
hours apart,
marathon sessions,
all-star games,
in shower stalls,
against hotel windows,
on backyard tables.

While our wedding bands
are no leather hoods,
our ice cream shop
has served flavors
beyond vanilla.

The kinkiest thing of all
is feeling wanted.

GALILEE AT DUSK

With names like Camelot and
Western Pines, we walled ourselves
into looped streets with neighborhood parks,
backyard grills and old refrigerators
full of beer cans magnetized
to teenage hands. We sat
in our motionless cars
before our sixteenth birthdays,
listening, in the dark,
to girls singing behind bedroom doors,
or, more interesting to boys like me,
the whist of their older brothers' hands
moving swiftly behind parted curtains.
This is life in your country, on sidewalks
in ten thousand American towns,
where two best friends linger
in the cul-de-sac smells
of frying chicken and tumbling laundry,
somebody's husband out front
sneaking a smoke, blowing rings
that rise to the high branches
of pine trees. One holds his eyes
on the other for a moment too long,
three timid breaths beyond
a mother's porchlit call,
proof that all of us answer
to voices other than our own.

MORNING COFFEE

I missed you like summer
to a frostbitten
finger.

Yes,
I missed you like a limb
lost to the jaws
of an alarm clock.

I missed you like
the spoiled flesh of young love
aches
in the haze of separation,
and though our divorce was to be permanent,
your custody of my consciousness
left me in a world of constant dark.

What good is a poet
without a cup of something?

Wine
in the evening,
or in the nearing dawn when creation stretches long,
but an early-hours citizen of a
Decaffei-Nation
I am not.

Returning to you,
carried like Cleopatra
on the able-bodied shoulders of your aroma,
you are again the warm sunlight
on my nearly withered leaves;
my steaming mug of photosynthesis
with a little
cream and sugar.

EULOGY TO MY TWENTIES

There goes the decade that fucked us both, Brother,
the twenties,
the gay twenties,
the roaring twenties,
the decade where you died and I was born,
twenty one, the cursed,
good riddance to naive sex,
to ignorant blisslessness,
to burying one's head in the ground,
to youth.
There goes the decade that
wouldn't go away.
What's more awkward than twenty three?
Perhaps twenty five, perhaps twenty seven.
Take these years and be gone,
they always said I looked sixteen,
each and every one.
Bring me to the age of adulthood and Jesus in his tomb,
the crest and crucifixion of life, spread lewdly and
on display,
the end of excuses and flexibility,
just take these years and be gone
with a dramatic farewell kiss in the July wind.
Twenty nine, I shed no tears for you,
now go. Become extinct.
Leave me with these aches and pains,
this confidence and peace,
leave me for the second half or third,
gallivant off merrily
to screw with someone else.

WE ARE EVERYWHERE AND NOWHERE

There are those of us
apathetic to the cause,
content with second-class citizenship
so long as the song never stops.

There are those of us
who are idealists,
barely tasting
the bitterness of defeat,
instead savoring
society's coronation,
thinking
if yes he can,
and yes he did,
then yes we shall,
eventually.

There are those of us
who march at the foot
of unholy fortresses,
hungry for blood and recognition,
cameras magnetized
to our rhymed chanting
and angry but fabulous faces.

There are those of us
who are your neighbors,
your colleagues,
your brothers and sisters,
your children now and yet to be.

We are the incarnation of battles won and lost.

We are everywhere and nowhere
simultaneously.

 99

WE PLANTED THESE TREES BY HAND

Dumbass One asks the questions
I hear most, *Which one is the woman?*
Which one do you call Ma?

I ask him back, *Which one of your parents takes it*
from behind? Dumbasses Two and Three turn like wolves,
growling laughter. I get this, mostly from the guys,

girls, sometimes, too, when they travel
in packs and sharpen their teeth on anything
different: longer socks, new haircut, two dads.

I can see it in their eyes, though, jealous of my solid pair
to their awkward four, to their bickering three,
to their lonely one and weekend visitation; no stepmonsters

in my house, just footballs and violins, rooms full
of the smell of baking bread and used books. I can name
the last 20 Secretaries of State. My batting average

is .385. I know my home wasn't created
by a six-pack and a busted rubber. My folks fought
for me. Who fought you into existence?

HYMN

It had been a while since we listened
to the stereo, that long-quiet thing

humming in the corner, forgotten
like a furnace in the summer months,

then it started snowing in our living room,
chilled wine glasses and half-empty beer mugs

frosty cold, so we cranked it up and
danced for warmth.

There were times when
these speakers were my religion,

between little deaths or the blind of a winter storm,
vocals, drums, guitar my holy trinity,

the oddest songs playing
with unplanned first kisses or perfect

like tonight, when I prayed
and the gods came down to sing.

DESCENDANTS OF LAZARUS
on the death of Nicholas Hughes, son of Sylvia Plath

My birth and your death
marked the only acts of love somewhat tangible,
though I admittedly remember neither,
one, bringing me to the life you could not bear, and
two, sealing our room before you suffocated yourself,
both subject to debate
on their inclusion herein.

I can ask you now, Mother,
did you save or condemn me?
Seventeen years I outlasted you,
in months, two hundred and four.
I was never the poet, often fighting
the urge to scribble nonsensical nothings,
gypsy genetics spiting me,
producing unwanted metaphor
I muttered and held under my breath
then swallowed and re-digested,
such toxic pills of heredity.

Instead I identified myself the scientist,
preferring facts proven cold or warm,
lists to stanzas, prime numbers
to melodramatic kidnappings
of the English language,
a rough and sturdy rope to the hugging heat of an oven.

One, my age, and
two, my sweet sister's.
The world has always had more of you
than we were allowed.
Did you intend to taunt me

with 'Lady Lazarus'?
Once each decade
you rose from the dead
until your legs no longer tried
but you could not survive another death
in the decade of us?

I made it so I could not fail,
the knot, too tight,
and in this,
Mother,
I bested you,
using the talents you gifted me
in those last instances of love or damnation
when you made me, when you left me,
so that sometime in the future,
the future becoming moments ago,
I could destroy to create this reunion,
when I took steps and counted,

one and then
two.

IF RIVER PHOENIX HAD LIVED

When I saw you in movies after *Stand by Me*
it was like you'd been resurrected,
though it felt like I was cheating the universe,
that I wasn't supposed to watch you grow older.
When you first disappeared to a haunting instrumental
of that title song, I mourned you. The second time,
I'd been robbed again, your beautiful face
crushed against the LA pavement
while a thunderstorm played paparazzi
and punk angels sang you to sleep.
If you had lived, your home would be lined with
golden statuettes. I picture them weeping
from roles others have played,
a gay cowboy or tragic rock god.
The internet is a viper, room
for a photograph of your open casket
and stories of those thieving seizures.
I'll remember you as Chris Chambers,
walking away, vanishing from sight,
never more perfect than at twelve years old,
Jesus, is anyone?

RAPTURE
for Christopher

I miss you during takeoff
where it has been my routine to
breathe you like an oxygen mask,
to plant my fingers firmly on the
solid ground of your forearms.
Without you
the runway is a marathon
long as life,
a cross country flight just to get in the air.
I drink ginger ale to calm my turbulence.
They've done away with free peanuts,
now they're five dollars, skyway robbery.
I'd rather spend the money on
anti-anxiety medication
and a souvenir for you.

IN DEFENSE OF EXISTENCE

On the east and west coasts,
homosexuality has been done to death.
Art (and marriage) reserved for procreation,
not reinterpretation of old headlines
or poems that chronicle the fading
hues of red ribbons laying dormant
in the bedside tables of Hollywood.
No one cares about coming out, children
rattle off their orientations from the crib
these days, but there are parts
of this country where nooses sway
from trees whose branches burn
in frontyard crucifixions and
God still hates faggots. In these places
we still live in quiet fear,
Casper, Wyoming, Walnut Ridge, Arkansas,
Troy, Alabama, where white sheets
and other masks hang in closets
side by side and it remains
courageous to whisper the word *pride*.

In the middle of America,
where the sun is just beginning to shine,
where stories literally die to be heard,
our young soldiers wander through rural wars
in heartland jungles while Fire Island queens
dance in the streets and critics proclaim
no need to voice our lives, we are strong
and growing stronger but
we are only as strong as our weak,
only as bright as the prism skin
of a Montana farmboy who
takes pills and swallows his tongue
rather than tell his father he's gay.

ADAM'S MANIFESTO ONE: SHAKE

I want to write until my hands bleed,
metaphors and sestinas,
wipe the sweat from my forehead
then turn the salty dampness that lingers
into a sonnet
about your skin and my lips.

I want to be forever
like Ginsberg and Whitman,
bring the beautiful darkness
into the light
and tell the boy
who, with the guilty fingerings,
remembers a touch, a simple brush of the shoulder,
that he is not damned to hell or loneliness.

I want my words to shatter myths and
create fantasy,
to be a temporary god
to a permanent atheist.

I want my poems
to cover you like bathwater,
for us to sink naked to intimate depths together.

I want these lines
to become songs sung by
young men with flushed faces and devilish intentions.

I want to take verbs
and thrust them, roughly,
into your hungry ego.

I want to take your hand and dance with you
alongside couplets that rhyme your creativity
with the displaced and triumphant loves of my life.

I want to be read in closets by flashlight
long after midnight.

I want to burst through closed doors
and bring heat
to your cold showers.

I want to force you
to wipe the steam from the mirror
and see yourself
as I would see you.

I want to lay my pen down
and let you pick it up, begin to write,
and change the world.

I want to shake things up.

ADAM'S MANIFESTO TWO: NEWSWORTHY

I write poetry from Small Town, Arkansas,
where my throbbing words
stab through your standards,
where my songs leap like dirty children
from trailerpark to trailerpark
where women gossip, shocked
and appalled on the worn heels
of Bud Light hiccups
in watercooler towns
where dry-thighed secretaries
cry God Almighty!
there's homosexuals among us
and they dare to live and love,
to work, to pray, to cry
to fuck, to have history,
and then dare to write about it?
Prying eyes, welcome here,
same as friend or foe or lover or ghost,
those who scan these pages
line by syllable, hoping
for something front-page worthy,
illiterate of the past,
knowing not it's old news,
my heroes were put on trial:
Ginsberg's magnificent "Howl"
smelled filthy and obscene,
Whitman's "Leaves of Grass"
left your men hiding erections.
You want the beautiful immoral,
read "Thomas" by Vytautas Pliura.
You want poetic orgasm, taste
"Blueberries" by Kirk Read.
If you want a sexually-monstrous mind
ask Dennis Cooper to dance
or peer into your husband's frontal lobe.

I've been around enough to know
art is supposed to shake you
art is supposed to bend you over
and dominate and leave you walking
slowly and off balance.
Art compels me
to beg, on my knees,
let me take your pen
and with its poisoned point
carve deep into my cheeks
marks of war
for I am limp wristed
and battle scarred, yes,
but limp wristed and battle scarred
with grenade in hand
throwing bombs of verb and pronoun
and scandalous adjective
but it's you who take these strings
of sin and syntax
into backrooms and gutters
as I profess my love
or humanity, for conflict, for dic
tionaries, it's you
who feel something stir within,
sticky and sweet and lingering
even after you decide to swallow,
and to those who feign distaste
at lyrical erotica and heart-blood splattered
and stained pixilated screens
and gasp
and throw forearms dramatically
against foreheads
covered with discount-store makeup,
I am the dark parts
of your bargain-bin religion
but with each click of the key
with each jolt of anger I send

to seethe your soul
I become more and more
what I want to be,
the maestro of metaphor,
the composer of controversy,
to you I am the devil
but them, I am
David and Goliath
locked in a torrid embrace,
a passionate spit-filled kiss,
I am Moses standing naked on the mountaintop,
my songs etched in stone,
and to my audience I sing
in a voice strong and confident,
proclaiming, commanding:
I have not yet begun to write.

MARK'S BIRTHDAY

After two pints of Guinness I announced
to the strangers and friends celebrating
Mark's birthday that my test came back

negative. The guys clapped and there were
high fives but one pulled me aside and asked
Would you have done the same if you were positive?

Ashamed through my buzz, I couldn't believe
I'd forgotten Austin and Tony and Dave. I couldn't
believe I'd walked into a room full of black men

and announced I was white, a room full of
Christians and announced I was atheist. I *do not*
see us as separate. I would kiss Tony on the lips

and have Dave in my home, but even these things
sound suspiciously similar to *I'm no racist;
I have Asian friends*. That night, at the table,

my relief was the sea that made us unequal.
I rode my own stupid waves of exoneration
from sexual ignorance to social bliss

and could not pretend the boys weren't drowning,
some of them. I was too quick to avoid hands
that could have pulled me in the poison;

just as thankful for forgiving friends
as I was for the dumb luck that accompanied
too many rubberless fucks.

THE BOOK OF BRADLEY

I will never be a father or an older brother
but that day I was both, a high school junior
giving the keys to you, barely 13, barely tall enough

to see over the dash of my Ford Mustang. You would
have been fine on those country backroads
had the sheriff not appeared in the rearview,

had you not lifted your foot and slowed to a crawl,
had you not been a highway toddler in irresponsible care,
then blue lights, of course, and we died together

as he walked to the driver's side, ticket pad in hand,
but when he saw you he laughed and said
don't let cops scare you, boy.

We tell this story over beers
on your 27th birthday. I am 31.
You have your beard and guitar. I have

my husband. I have never loved you more
than this moment. I have never better understood
what I've missed, what I've had.

REVELATIONS

Walt Whitman's notes reveal masculine darlings redressed
in fabrics of femininity, blatant homosexuality erased

from history and reincarnated into the kind eyes
of a counselor who listened as I said *I think I'm gay.*

He shook his head and told me intelligent people
are more adventurous in bed. He prescribed

a punching bag to pummel temptation, a *Playboy*
to redirect the flow of blood to somewhere

more acceptable. My knuckles bruised as we
hit walls, five weeks, then six without success.

He shook my hand and told me to call him
when I was ready to put in the effort. Instead

I logged into gay.com and made a lunch date
with the cutest boy I'd ever seen.

AN OUTSIDER'S GUIDE TO GAY MARRIAGE

Monday he wakes me after he showers
with a hand on my stomach. He smells
like soap and coffee. Tuesday he cuts
the grass. I meet him at the door with water,
towel the sweat from his forehead.
On Wednesday we sit on the sofa,
my feet on his lap. We watch too many
hours of reality television, then go
to bed early. On Thursday, I show him
again the easiest way to chop an onion.
I make chicken soup, he cleans the dishes.
We fold laundry and play with our cats.
On Friday, we meet after work
for dinner. It is date night; we talk
about the week and plan our grocery list.
Saturday morning we sleep late. I indulge
myself in his warmth, feel protected
in his orbit. Then it is Sunday,
more chores around the house,
our schedules built to end the day
with *Desperate Housewives* and a plate
full of food, the same as every
other house on the block.

MOTHER-IN-LAW

That first year, your mother was Debbie
from *Queer as Folk*. I couldn't
think of her otherwise, red-headed, brassy.

She would call
during every date. It
was a good son's duty to answer.

Once, when you weren't looking,
I turned off your phone. An hour later,
she knocked on our door.

I invited her in for breakfast
and began the balancing act
every man has to learn.

RESURRECTION

Three religious leaders,
a Southern Baptist preacher,
a rabbi, and a female minister
walked into a gay bar.

You have to understand the significance.

In Arkansas, we worship at the club
on Saturday night. In Arkansas,
the blood of the lamb
is a gin and tonic. In Arkansas,
we pray to angels in drag
and slide dollars in their
tucked and taped collection plates.

In Arkansas, we're going to hell.

Wait a second,
said the preacher,
coincidentally black,
coincidentally wearing the same cloth
of the church of guilt I grew up in,
Jesus never mentioned homosexuality.
Jesus preached love.
Jesus would have been here
with a drink in his hand.

Sodom and Gomorra? said the Rabbi,
That wasn't about God's wrath
on the gay man. That was about
the repercussions of inhospitality.
The hero in that story

offered his daughters to be raped;
his daughters seduced him.
This is the story used to nail you
to the cross?

The female minister cried
as she told of being forced away
from a congregation
when she got the calling to spread
God's word. Now she said
I've got my own church. I'll bless
your relationships. I won't ask
for permission.

You have to understand
we were in Little Rock, Arkansas.
The room was full of men and woman
abused as children and adults
by Sunday school teachers
and classroom coaches who spelled
Jesus H-A-T-E and sacrificed us
like our names were Isaac.
All we wanted
was to be Daddy's little girls
and boys.

In our neighborhoods
we hate religion
like religion hates us.

That night the best of religion
apologized
and although we still aren't sure

(we are battered wives, after all)
the wounds on our spirit
began to scab over.

Maybe now,
when we pass on the street,
we'll nod politely
instead of throwing fire.

Remember, said the preacher,
He that loves his brother abides in the light.

ABOUT THE POET

Bryan Borland lives in Arkansas with his husband, Christopher Baxter. *My Life as Adam* is his first full-length collection. Visit him online at www.bryanborland.com.

ABOUT THE ARTIST

Seth Ruggles Hiler is a realist at heart and an expressionist in soul. His influences range from Giotto and Rembrandt to Diebenkorn and Lucian Freud. Whether he is painting a portrait, landscape, still life, or the figure within nature, Seth's main goal is to express the emotional impact of what he observes. He translates these images through a variety of media including oils, acrylics, gouache, and graphite. Seth's portrait, "Aaron," which appears as the cover of *My Life as Adam*, is part of his "Twenty-Something" body of work, a series of paintings of men in their twenties. To learn more about Seth, to view or purchase his work, or to commission a painting or drawing, visit his website at www.sethruggleshiler.com.

ABOUT THE PUBLISHER

The mission of Sibling Rivalry Press is to develop, publish, and promote outlaw artistic talent—those projects which inspire people to read, challenge, and ponder the complexities of life in dark rooms, under blankets by cell-phone illumination, in the backseats of cars, and on spring-day park benches next to people reading Plath, Ginsberg, and Whitman. We welcome manuscripts which push boundaries, sing sweetly, or inspire us to perform karaoke in drag. Not much makes us flinch.

WWW.SIBLINGRIVALRYPRESS.COM